Chocolate

Savor The Flavor

Elaine Landau

THE ROURKE PRESS, INC.
VERO BEACH, FLORIDA 32964

PHOTO CREDITS
Ben Klaffke

EDITORIAL SERVICES
Editorial Directions Inc.

Library of Congress Cataloging-in-Publication Data

Landau, Elaine.
    Chocolate : savor the flavor / Elaine Landau.
        p. cm. — (Tasty treats)
    Includes bibliographical references.
    Summary: Provides an introduction to chocolate, describing its history and some of the forms in which it is enjoyed.
    ISBN 1-57103-336-X
    1. Chocolate—Juvenile literature. [1. Chocolate.] I. Title.

TX767.C5 L28 2000
641.3'374—dc21

                                                                    00–022392

Printed in the USA

AEB-5420

Contents

Chocolate 5

Chocolate History 7

It Starts with a Tree 11

The Lowdown on Chocolate 16

Chocolate Fun Facts 19

Glossary 22

For Further Reading 23

Index 24

Chocolate

Bite into a piece of chocolate. Savor the flavor. People around the world love it.

Americans spend millions of dollars on chocolate. There are countless kinds of chocolate candies. There is also chocolate cake, pudding, and soda.

There are many ways to enjoy chocolate. Chocolate ice cream sodas are delicious.

How about chocolate ice cream and chocolate **syrup**? You can probably think of many other ways chocolate is eaten. If you want to know more about this popular treat, keep reading.

Chocolate History

There is nothing new about chocolate. By the 1500s, the **Aztec** Indians in Mexico enjoyed it. They made a liquid chocolate drink. It was called "chocolatl," which meant warm liquid. Chocolatl was a little like hot cocoa.

Chocolatl was a bit like the cocoa shown here.

Only Aztec royalty drank chocolate. Even they saved it for special occasions. The drink was served at weddings, baptisms, and festivals.

Later on, Spanish explorers came to Mexico. They took chocolate home with them. The Spaniards sweetened it with sugar cane. Before long, the drink became popular throughout Europe.

In 1847, an English company made chocolate that could be chewed. Solid chocolate had been made before, but it was only used for cooking. The product had never before been smooth or sweet enough to eat.

Through the years chocolate has been greatly improved. Today, it is part of many desserts. You find it everywhere.

Can you imagine an ice cream store without chocolate ice cream? Or a candy store that sold jelly beans but did not have any you-know-what?

Ice cream chocolate sundae

Ice cream and chocolate are great together

It Starts with a Tree

Believe it or not, chocolate does not come from a box – or even from a factory. Chocolate begins with the **cacao** bean. Cacao beans grow in pods on cacao trees. These trees thrive in warm, wet climates.

A Malaysian woman holding cacao pods.

They grow in West Africa. Cacao trees are also found in Brazil, Equador, Mexico, Trinidad, and the Dominican Republic.

The ripe cacao pods are picked, and the beans removed. The beans are then dried in the sun.

Here cacao beans are dried in the sun before being placed in a sack.

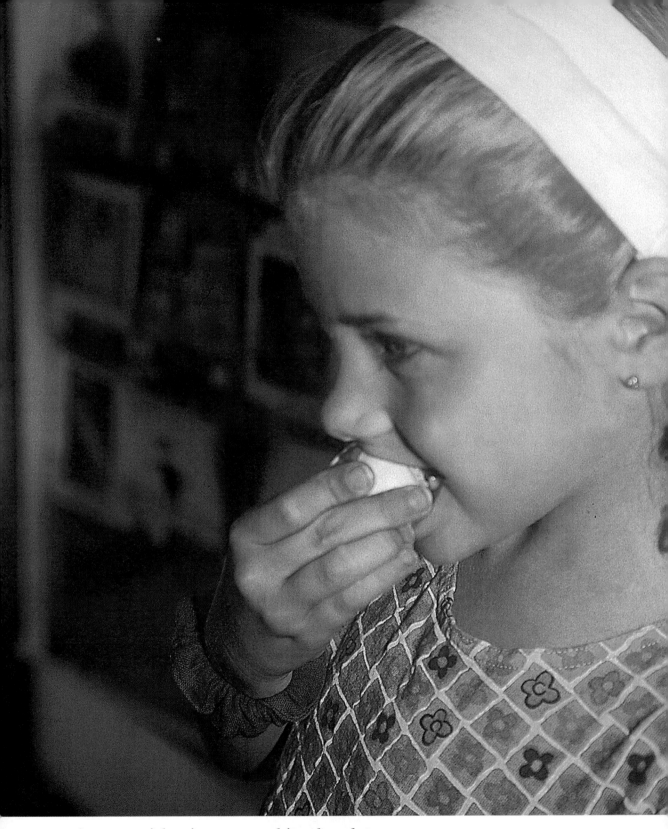

A young girl enjoys some white chocolate

Finally they are shipped to factories around the world to be made into chocolate.

Various chocolate products are made. There are, however, three types of "eatable" chocolate. These are milk chocolate, dark chocolate, and white chocolate. Which is your favorite?

Americans eat a tremendous amount of all kinds of chocolate.

The Lowdown on Chocolate

You may have heard a lot about chocolate. But is it all true?

Chocolate has often been blamed for tooth **decay**. Yet it is no worse for teeth than other sugary foods. Frequent brushing and regular visits to the dentist will help prevent decay.

Are you ready for a surprise? Chocolate also contains healthy things. A milk chocolate bar has protein, calcium, and iron in it. It also has carbohydrates. **Carbohydrates** are a good source of energy for sports and other activities. There is usually room for a little chocolate in a well-balanced diet.

Brushing after sweets helps prevent tooth decay.

Chocolate **Fun Facts**

 Cacao beans were highly prized in ancient times. The Aztecs sometimes used them as money.

 The Hershey chocolate factory in Hershey, Pennsylvania, is the world's largest chocolate plant. It is large enough to cover the floor of the Houston Astrodome five times.

 More than 2½ billion pounds of chocolate are eaten in the United States each year.

 The most frequently purchased item at movie candy counters is chocolate-covered raisins.

A young baseball player eats a chocolate ice cream pop for extra energy

Hershey's chocolate kisses at the factory.

Chocolate covered raisins are a favorite at the movies.

Glossary

Aztec (AZ tek) – an ancient Indian tribe from
  Mexico

cacao (kuh KAW) – the tree from which chocolate
  is made

carbohydrates (kar boh HYE drates) – foods that
  supply the body with energy

decay (di KAY) – to rot or weaken

syrup (SUR uhp) – a thick, sweet, flavored liquid

For Further Reading

Kalbacken, Joan. *The Food Pyramid.* Danbury, Connecticut: Children's Press, 1998.

Landau, Elaine. *Sugar.* Danbury, Connecticut: Children's Press, 1999.

Llewellyn, Claire. *What's for Lunch?* Chocolate. Danbury, Connecticut: Children's Press, 1998.

Rockwell, Lizzy. *Good Enough to Eat.* New York: HarperCollins, 1999

Index

Aztec Indians   7

cacao bean   11, 12

carbohydrates   16

chocolate-covered raisins   19, 21

chocolatl   7, 8

desserts   8

flavor   5

sugar cane   8

tooth decay   16